Cape May's Gingerbread Gems

Tina Skinner

Photography by Bruce Waters and Tina Skinner

Schiffer Publishing Ltd ®

4880 Lower Valley Road, Atglen, PA 19310 USA

Front cover photo:

On the cover: The Abbey, 34 Gurney Street, c. 1869-70. The sixty-foot tower makes this home a standout in the city. It is Gothic Revival style, typified by steeply pitched roofs, hood molds over the windows, designed by Stephen Decatur Button for a wealthy coal baron as his summer home.

Title page photo:

The Brass Bed Inn, 719 Columbia Avenue, c. 1872. Gothic Revival with bump-out sunroom over flat verandah roof. The earth tone pigments – high-gloss and matte yellow with green and red accents – are indicative of colors available when the home was first built.

Endsheet photo:

Chalfonte Hotel, Howard and Sewell Streets, c. 1876. American Bracketed Villa with Italianate decorative elements. Civil War hero Colonel Henry Sawyer may have fought for the North, but the hotel he built and operated exudes Southern charm and hospitality.

Published by Schiffer Publishing Ltd.
4880 Lower Valley Road
Atglen, PA 19310
Phone: (610) 593-1777; Fax: (610) 593-2002
E-mail: Info@schifferbooks.com

For the largest selection of fine reference books on this and related subjects, please visit our web site at
www.schifferbooks.com
We are always looking for people to write books on new and related subjects. If you have an idea for a book please contact us at the above address.

This book may be purchased from the publisher.
Include $3.95 for shipping.
Please try your bookstore first.
You may write for a free catalog.

In Europe, Schiffer books are distributed by
Bushwood Books
6 Marksbury Ave.
Kew Gardens
Surrey TW9 4JF England
Phone: 44 (0) 20 8392-8585; Fax: 44 (0) 20 8392-9876
E-mail: info@bushwoodbooks.co.uk
Free postage in the U.K., Europe; air mail at cost.

Copyright © 2005 by Schiffer Publishing, Ltd.
Library of Congress Control Number: 2004105860

Designed by "Sue"
Type set in Allegro BT/Aldine 721 Lt BT

ISBN 0-7643-2126-9
Printed in China

Preface

Dear Reader,

We've worked hard to double check facts, dates, and names, and hope you will help us. Please forward any errors or ommissions in writing so that we might incorporate these changes into our next edition. Thank you for your support.

The Author & Editors

Introduction

As the first and oldest shore resort in the United States, the pretty little town of Cape May draws an estimated twenty million visitors annually. This National Historic Landmark City offers fine beaches, exciting restaurants and tree-shaded streets lined with Victorian homes and shops. In all, more than 600 restored Victorian structures stand in this petite city, all easily accessed by a day's walk.

A major fire destroyed thirty-five acres of Cape May's wooden architecture in 1878. The town was rebuilt, most in the fanciful, ornamented styles that typified the time and attract people to Victorian style today. Three famous architects played a leading role in the rebuilding: Frank Furness, Samuel Sloan, and Stephen Decatur Button. Their talents, paired with the timely invention of the jigsaw, resulted in the city's thick population of heavily ornamented cottages and mansions.

In 1967, the city undertook its Victorian District Urban Renewal Project, tearing down hopelessly dilapidated structures and giving the rest a new lease on life. The town was designated a "Historic District" on the National Register of Historic Places in 1976, ready to deliver when the Americans became enamored with all things Victorian in the 1980s.

Ashley Rose Victorian Inn, 715 Columbia Avenue, c. 1872-73. Designed by Stephen Decatur Button in the Cape Gothic style. A creative paint job marries feminine summer colors with the institution's poetic name. The colorful inn has appeared in *Life Magazine* and *National Geographic*.

Opposite page:
Mainstay Inn, 635 Columbia Avenue, c. 1872. Italianate Villa designed by Stephen Decatur Button in a style reminiscent of antebellum architecture. Originally built as a gambling and entertainment club for gentlemen, it later housed naval officers and their families stationed in Cape May during World War I.

Delsea Hotel, 621 Columbia Avenue, c. 1867. Candy cane Corinthian columns and dental moulding are among the finer details of gingerbread appliqués on this historic cottage.

The Mason Cottage Bed & Breakfast, 625 Columbia Avenue, c. 1871. Built as a private summer residence by Edward A. Warne, a wealthy Philadelphia entrepreneur. The Warne family sold the "cottage" to the Mason family in the mid-1940s. The Mason's have maintained the building's original shade of off-white and even restored much of the original furniture.

The Stockton Cottages, or Stockton Place Row Houses, Gurney Street. Gothic Revival cottages originally built as rentals in 1869. The Stockton Row cottages were a summer retreat for wealthy families who, together with their servants and nannies, would travel from Philadelphia and Virginia to summer in Cape May.

Opposite page:
Summer Cottage Inn, 613 Columbia Avenue, c. 1867. Commissioned to be built by S. A. Harrison as a family summer vacation cottage. Philadelphia Architect Stephen Decatur Button created this Italianate style home complete with cupola.

Mooring Guest House, 801 Stockton Avenue, 1882. One of Cape May's few bed and breakfast inns originally built as a guesthouse, designed to accommodate the fashionable Victorian on seaside holiday.

Opposite page:
839 Kearney Avenue. This classic Second Empire style home is topped by a Mansard roof and prettied by the curve of a veranda and arched accent windows.

Morning Star Villa, 1307 Beach Drive, c. 1884-85. A star motif is repeated in mouldings and gingerbread applications. But for the fourth floor, a later edition, this home is classic Second Empire style.

Joseph Leedom House, Congress and Lafayette Streets, c. 1887. Queen Anne style typified by asymmetrical massing of various architectural elements and a mix of finishes. A pair of towers adds impressive stature to a home, with unexpected dormers and porches adding interest and variety throughout the structure.

The Stockton Manor, 805 Beach Drive, c. 1872-73. Classic Second Empire style is apparent in the original block of the structure, with a mere suggestion of a protruding central pavilion. Later add-ons include a wrap-around veranda and additions to the rear.

Opposite page:
931 Beach Drive. Seemingly in search of Second Empire style, with the Mansard roof and a projecting central pavilion, this building strayed from symmetry with the addition of a three-story tower.

902 Washington Street. Pink, white, and picket fence typify the charm and allure of rural Victorian architecture.

Opposite page:
May Caper, 815 Beach Drive. This little Gothic cottage typifies the eclectic and asymmetrical nature of the architectural style.

Baronet, 819 Beach Drive. This ocean-front home is symmetrical in all details.

Opposite page:
Cape Scape, 933 Beach Drive. A conical roof accentuates and unusual top line in this eclectic, ocean-front property.

921 Beach Drive. Bric-a-brac and turned rails adorn this ocean-front property.

Opposite page:
The Inn on the Ocean, E.D. Wolfe Cottage, 25 Ocean Street, c. 1880. Intricate cutout work on the railings and roof cresting are among the pretty details on this French Second Empire cottage. The pink fish-scale siding adds icing to the bracketed, straight mansard roof.

805 Stockton Avenue. "Mother Daughter" twin home, built in 1881.

Opposite page:
606 Columbia Avenue. Built by the same millionaire who commissioned the Abbey, this modest home served as summer getaway for his son. The home's elaborate railings and wrought iron roof work captivate the eye.

The Empress, formerly Bell Shields House, Decatur and Hughes Streets. Pretty colors and the sheer immensity of this stick style dwelling leave a lasting impression.

Opposite page:
Beauclaire's, 23 Ocean Street, c. 1879. Classic Queen Anne style – asymmetrical with a medley of architectural elements including a conical roof over the tower. Five original leaded glass windows are a true treat. Wallis Warfield, later the Duchess of Windsor, summered here according to local lore.

The Christopher Gallagher House, 45 Jackson Street, c. 1882-83. Identical to Poor Richard's Inn (following) with an extended porch. The Second Empire style emphasizes perfect symmetry at each of the three levels.

Opposite page:
Poor Richard's Inn, 17 Jackson Street, c. 1882. Perfect example of Second Empire, with mansard roof and exacting symmetry. Restoration work included replacement of 1,600 pieces of multi-colored roof slate.

The Seven Sisters, 10-20 Jackson Street, c. 1891-92. Seven identical homes open to a private courtyard (Atlantic Terrace) and were designed by Stephen Decatur Button. These tightly contained cubes imitate sixteenth century urban Italian homes, though the light gingerbread and molding applications are more typical of the town than the architectural form.

Opposite page:
45 Jackson Street. A towering Second Empire leaves no one guessing with its greatly projected central pavilion, in this case used as porch and balcony.

33 Perry Street. An appropriately pink bridal shop, Uniquely Yours, is located on the first floor of this elaborately trimmed, three-tiered "wedding cake" of a Gothic Revival house. Naturally, the business specializes in Victorian weddings.

The Merry Widow, formerly J. Henry Edmonds House, 42 Jackson Street, c. 1879. The curved porch accentuates the curve of the building's tower, built-in to the straight mansard roofline of a modified Queen Anne castle-ette. The witch's hat tower cap presents a fanciful front-on view.

The Belmont, 712 Columbia Street, c. 1879. A polygonal chimney is one of the hall-marks of the Gothic Revival cottage, along with embellished hooded dormers in the steeply pitched roofs. In a town where most cottages have been retrofit with retractable awnings, this permanent awning has obvious advantages.

Opposite page:
The King's Cottage, 9 Perry Street, c. 1879. This stick-style cottage was designed by Philadelphia architect Frank Furness. The detail image shows ceramic tiles, which were

Southern Mansion, 700 Washington Street, 1863. Philadelphia industrialist George Allen commissioned this American bracket, post and beam villa, designed by the internationally acclaimed architect Samuel Sloan and constructed by Henri Phillipi. It is the largest and most opulent Cape May mansion, in the heart of the historic district.

Opposite page:
213 Perry Street. An artist was inspired to paint leaves on the front stair risers of this pretty, Gothic cottage.

John F. Craig House, 609 Columbia Avenue, Carpenter Gothic style inn.

Opposite page:
908 Stockton Avenue. Red fish-scale shingles and gingerbread trim adorn this simple cottage.

Dormer House, 800 Columbia Avenue at Franklin, c. 1899.

Opposite page:
The Albert Stevens Inn, 127 Myrtle Avenue, 1898 Queen Anne Victorian home. Commissioned as a wedding gift by Dr. Albert G. Stevens, a Cape May homeopathic medical doctor, for his bride, Bessie. The house was restored and converted to a bed and breakfast inn in 1980 when Vesta Stevens-Olsen, the only child of Albert and Bessie died and the house was sold to investors.

The Henry Sawyer Inn, 722 Columbia Street, c. 1877. The building was commissioned by Eldridge Johnson – treasurer of Cape May, president of the Cape May Savings and Building Association, and trustee of the Presbyterian Church; and built by Henry Sawyer – Cape May's Civil War hero, proprietor of the Chalfonte Hotel, and Cape May city councilman.

Opposite page:
Prickly Pear Cottage, 670 Welsh Street. This pretty Queen Anne style cottage is home to The Art League in Cape May. Two three-sided dormers add architectural interest to the building.

601 Columbia Avenue. This is one of the few remaining original Victorian storefronts in Cape May.

Opposite page:
Sugar Plum Cottage, 114 Decatur Street. The most expressively colorful home in Cape May, this one is like-named, as well.

The Queen Victoria Bed & Breakfast, 102 Ocean Street, c. 1881. An imposing block of building, this Second Empire style home is made graceful by the bell curves of the mansard roof, accentuated by a green and red color palette.

Opposite page:
The Joseph Hall House, 645 Hughes Street, c. 1868. A striking color combination highlights the intricate vergeboard.

Belvedere Condos, 101 Lafayette Street. Accent colors highlight the brackets and ornaments on this spacious Italianate style home.

Opposite page:
Franklin Hughes House, 665 Hughes Street. Wisteria softens the façade of this gaily painted, Gothic Revival private residence.

203 Congress Place. This Italianate mansion presents a formidable three-floor front to passersby.

Opposite page:
John Wesley Inn, 30 Gurney Street, c. 1869. Carpenter Gothic restored precisely to its original condition by the Tice family, owners since 1983.

130 Decatur Street, c. 1895. A prominent brow or arch over this window, and a tower with pyramidal roof are among the architectural features that distinguish this small domicile.

124 Decatur Street. A snug yellow Second Empire home is iced with olive and brick red trim.

The Goodman House, 118 Decatur Street. A dollhouse and miniature museum occupy this happy blue and yellow themed Victorian. Next door, pink and white make a pretty partnership.

Opposite page:
Dr. Henry L. Hunt House, 209 Congress Place, c. 1881. AThis private home sports it all – mansard rooflines punctuated by steep-pitched dormer bump-outs typical of Gothic Revival, and a Queen Anne conical roof. Stick-style trim is set alongside elaborate gingerbread. The belvedere is the largest example of a lookout pavilion in town.

Opposite page:
Judson Bennett House, 835 Washington Street, c. 1882. A jaunty tower and second floor overhangs add to the architectural variety of a Queen Anne style home.

Right:
Inn at 22 Jackson Street, c. 1899. A flashy coat of paint brings out the best in this feature-packed Queen Anne style home. Exterior assets include clusters of elaborate turned porch columns and a jaunty octagonal tower topped by a "witch's hat" conical roof.

613 Columbia Avenue, and Pharo's, 617 Columbia Avenue, designed by Stephen Decatur Button. These two matching Italianate buildings make a pretty pair, their differences a point of contemplation from the street.

Opposite page:
210 Congress Street. Steep roof angles belie the rounded face this residence presents to passersby.

The Inn of Cape May, Beach Drive and Ocean Street, c. 1894. This imposing Queen Ann style hotel is crowned by twin tent roofs. In 1917, Wallis Warfield, later the Duchess of Windsor, had her "coming out" party here.

Opposite page:
The Linda Lee Bed and Breakfast, formerly the John Benezet Cottage, 725 Columbia Avenue, c. 1872. A pair of pointed windows are central gems on this Carpenter Gothic.

Angel of the Sea Inn, 5-7 Trenton Street, c. 1850. Built as a "summer cottage" for Philadelphia chemist William Weightman, Sr., this was originally a single building that stood on the corner of Franklin and Washington Streets until 1881. It was cut it in half when moved closer to the ocean, but the local carpenters found they couldn't push it together again.

Opposite page:
Leith Hall, 22 Ocean Street. This Second Empire wears a wonderful striped-awning skirt.

107 Ocean Street. Fish-scale shingles and clapboard add variety to a classic Gothic cottage.

Opposite page:
Celtic Inn, 24 Ocean Street. A small Second Empire has a new life as a bed and breakfast.

Fairthorne Bed and Breakfast, 111 Ocean Street. A Queen Anne style home, this cottage now doubles as an inn with the house next door.